Spam: How To Keep Your Marketing Emails In The Inbox

Roy Hendershot

Published by Roy Hendershot, 2024.

SPAM: HOW TO KEEP YOUR MARKETING EMAILS IN THE INBOX

First edition. June 14, 2024.

Written by Roy Hendershot.

Table of Contents

Chapter 1: Understanding Email Spam Filters

———

Email spam filters are like digital bouncers at a club, deciding which emails get in and which are shown the door. They sift through millions of emails every day, picking out the ones that look suspicious or unwanted. This process is vital because no one wants their inbox flooded with junk. Spam filters use a combination of rules and algorithms to identify spammy emails. They look at everything from the subject line to the content, links, and even the sender's reputation. Understanding how these filters work can help you craft emails that get through.

Spam filters weren't always this sophisticated. Back in the early days of the internet, spam was rampant because there weren't many rules in place. As email usage grew, so did the problem of spam. This led to the development of basic spam filters that used simple rules to block obvious junk mail. Over time, these filters have evolved, becoming more complex and effective. Nowadays, they use advanced techniques, including machine learning, to keep up with the ever-changing tactics of spammers.

When an email gets flagged as spam, it usually ends up in a special folder where it's unlikely to be seen. This is bad news for marketers because it means their carefully crafted messages go unnoticed. To avoid this fate, it's essential to understand why emails get flagged in the first place. Common reasons include using certain trigger words, sending from a suspicious IP address, and having a poor sender reputation. Knowing these pitfalls can help you avoid them.

The importance of staying out of the spam folder can't be overstated. When your emails are marked as spam, it affects your entire email marketing strategy. Not only do your messages go unread, but your sender reputation also takes a hit. This can make it even harder to get your emails delivered in the future. By understanding and avoiding the common causes of spam flags, you can improve your chances of reaching your audience.

Major email service providers like Gmail, Yahoo, and Outlook each have their own spam filtering systems. While they share some common principles, each has unique criteria and algorithms. This means an email that passes through one provider's filters might get flagged by another. Understanding the nuances of each provider's system can help you tailor your emails to meet their specific requirements, increasing your overall deliverability.

Artificial intelligence plays a significant role in modern spam filters. AI systems can analyze vast amounts of data and recognize patterns that would be impossible for humans to detect. They learn from past examples of spam and legitimate emails to improve their accuracy over time. This makes AI-powered spam filters incredibly effective at catching unwanted emails while letting genuine messages through. As a marketer, staying up-to-date with AI advancements can give you an edge in navigating these filters.

Case studies of successful email campaigns provide valuable insights into what works and what doesn't. For instance, a campaign that avoided common spam triggers and focused on engaging content had significantly higher open rates. These examples highlight the importance of understanding your audience and crafting messages that resonate with them. By studying successful campaigns, you can learn strategies that increase your chances of staying out of the spam folder.

Examples of emails that end up in spam often contain obvious red flags like all-caps subject lines, excessive punctuation, and too many links. They might also come from unfamiliar or suspicious domains. Analyzing these examples can teach you what to avoid in your own emails. It's crucial to strike a balance between catching your audience's attention and steering clear of spammy tactics.

Identifying spam trigger words is an essential part of crafting spam-free emails. Words like "free," "win," and "urgent" are common triggers that can raise red flags with spam filters. Instead of using these terms, find alternative ways to convey your message. This not only helps you avoid the spam folder but also makes your emails sound more genuine and engaging.

The impact of spam on marketing efforts is significant. When your emails don't reach your audience, it's like talking to an empty room. Your messages, offers, and updates go unnoticed, leading to missed opportunities and wasted resources. To make the most of your email marketing efforts, it's crucial to understand and avoid the factors that can lead to your emails being marked as spam.

There are many myths about email spam filters, such as the idea that including too many images will automatically get your email flagged. While certain practices can increase your chances of landing in the spam folder, it's not always a straightforward cause-and-effect situation. Spam filters consider multiple factors, and understanding the myths versus the realities can help you make better decisions when crafting your emails.

Common mistakes marketers make include using purchased email lists, sending too many emails, and neglecting to authenticate their sending domains. These practices can harm your sender reputation and increase the likelihood of your emails being marked as spam. By avoiding these mistakes, you can improve your email deliverability and build a stronger relationship with your audience.

There's a difference between the spam and promotions tabs in email clients like Gmail. While the promotions tab isn't as bad as the spam folder, emails that land there are still less likely to be seen. To maximize your email visibility, aim for the primary inbox by focusing on relevance and engagement. This means creating content that your audience finds valuable and wants to read.

Tools to test email deliverability can help you understand how your emails are performing and identify any issues that need addressing. These tools simulate how different email providers might handle your messages, giving you insights into potential problems. By regularly testing your emails, you can catch and fix issues before they impact your campaigns.

Spam filters are constantly updating to keep up with new spam tactics. What works today might not work tomorrow, so it's important to stay informed about the latest changes. Following industry blogs, participating in forums, and using up-to-date testing tools can help you stay ahead of the curve and keep your emails out of the spam folder.

The evolution of spam filtering technology has been driven by the need to protect users from an ever-growing volume of unwanted emails. From simple rule-based filters to advanced AI-powered systems, the technology has come a long way. Understanding this evolution can help you appreciate the complexities of modern spam filters and better navigate their challenges.

Analyzing your email deliverability rates involves looking at various metrics, such as open rates, click-through rates, and bounce rates. These metrics can give you insights into how well your emails are reaching your audience and where improvements are needed. Regular analysis helps you track your progress and make data-driven decisions to enhance your email marketing strategy.

Interpreting spam reports is crucial for understanding why your emails might be getting flagged. These reports provide detailed information about which aspects of your emails are problematic. By carefully reviewing these reports, you can identify and address issues, improving your chances of getting your emails delivered successfully.

The relationship between sender reputation and spam is critical. A good sender reputation means your emails are more likely to be delivered, while a poor reputation increases the chances of ending up in the spam folder. Maintaining a positive sender reputation requires consistent best practices, such as sending relevant content, managing your email list, and addressing spam complaints promptly.

Understanding blacklists is important for any email marketer. Blacklists are lists of IP addresses or domains known for sending spam. If your IP or domain gets blacklisted, your emails are likely to be blocked by many email providers. Knowing how blacklists work and how to avoid getting listed can help you protect your sender reputation and ensure your emails reach their intended recipients.

Avoiding getting blacklisted involves following best practices like not using purchased email lists, authenticating your sending domains, and keeping your email content relevant. If you do find yourself on a blacklist, there are steps you can take to get delisted, such as identifying and fixing the issue that caused the listing and submitting a request to the blacklist operator.

Real-life stories of companies affected by spam filters highlight the importance of good email practices. These stories often involve businesses that saw their email deliverability plummet due to mistakes like sending too many emails or failing to authenticate their domains. Learning from these examples can help you avoid similar pitfalls and improve your email marketing strategy.

Best practices for staying out of spam include using clear and concise subject lines, avoiding spam trigger words, personalizing your emails, and regularly cleaning your email list. By following these practices, you can increase your chances of getting your emails delivered to your audience's primary inbox, enhancing your email marketing efforts.

Now that we've explored the ins and outs of email spam filters, it's time to dive into another crucial aspect of email marketing: building a strong sender reputation. This chapter will guide you through the steps to establish and maintain a reputation that keeps your emails out of the spam folder and in front of your audience.

Chapter 2: Building a Strong Sender Reputation

A strong sender reputation is like having a good credit score for your emails. It's a measure of how trustworthy and reliable you are as a sender, based on various factors like your sending history, email engagement rates, and spam complaints. Just as a good credit score can help you get better interest rates, a strong sender reputation can improve your email deliverability, making it more likely that your messages will reach your audience's inboxes.

Several factors influence your sender reputation, including the quality of your email list, your sending frequency, and the content of your emails. For example, if you frequently send emails to invalid addresses or receive a lot of spam complaints, your reputation will suffer. On the other hand, if you send relevant and engaging content to a well-maintained list, your reputation will improve. Understanding these factors can help you take the necessary steps to build and maintain a strong sender reputation.

One of the first steps to building a strong sender reputation is checking your current reputation. There are various tools available that can help you assess your sender reputation, providing insights into your deliverability rates, spam complaints, and other relevant metrics. Regularly monitoring your reputation allows you to identify and address any issues before they become major problems.

IP addresses play a significant role in sender reputation. When you send an email, it's associated with the IP address of your sending server. If that IP address has a history of sending spam, your emails are more likely to be flagged as spam. This is why it's important to use a reputable email service provider that maintains clean IP addresses and monitors their sending practices to ensure they aren't being used for spam.

Domain reputation is also crucial. Unlike IP reputation, which is tied to the server's address, domain reputation is linked to your specific domain name. This means that even if you change email service providers, your domain reputation will follow you. Maintaining a good domain reputation involves sending relevant and engaging content, avoiding spammy practices, and regularly monitoring your reputation.

Consistency in your sending pattern is key to maintaining a strong sender reputation. Sudden spikes or drops in your sending volume can raise red flags with spam filters. Establishing a consistent sending schedule helps build trust with email providers, making it more likely that your emails will be delivered to your audience's inboxes.

Improving your sender reputation involves several strategies. First, focus on sending relevant and engaging content that your audience wants to receive. This not only improves your engagement rates but also reduces the likelihood of spam complaints. Second, regularly clean your email list to remove invalid addresses and inactive subscribers. Third, use authentication protocols like SPF, DKIM, and DMARC to verify your emails and protect against spoofing.

Email engagement has a direct impact on your sender reputation. High open rates, click-through rates, and low bounce rates signal to email providers that your emails are relevant and wanted. To improve engagement, focus on creating compelling subject lines, personalized content, and clear calls-to-action. Regularly testing different elements of your emails can also help you identify what resonates with your audience.

Increasing email engagement involves understanding your audience and tailoring your content to their interests and needs. Personalization is key here. By using data like past purchase behavior, browsing history, and demographic information, you can create emails that feel more relevant and engaging to your recipients. This not only improves engagement rates but also builds trust and loyalty with your audience.

Real-life examples of improved sender reputations can provide valuable insights. For instance, a company that focused on sending personalized and relevant content saw a significant increase in their open and click-through rates, leading to a stronger sender reputation. These examples highlight the importance of understanding your audience and continuously improving your email marketing strategy.

Handling spam complaints promptly and effectively is crucial for maintaining a strong sender reputation. When a recipient marks your email as spam, it sends a negative signal to email providers. Addressing these complaints involves identifying the cause, such as irrelevant content or too frequent emails, and making necessary adjustments to your strategy. It's also important to provide an easy way for recipients to unsubscribe, reducing the likelihood of spam complaints.

Authentication protocols like SPF, DKIM, and DMARC play a vital role in building a strong sender reputation. SPF (Sender Policy Framework) verifies that the email comes from an authorized server. DKIM (DomainKeys Identified Mail) adds a digital signature to your emails, ensuring they haven't been tampered with during transit. DMARC (Domain-based Message Authentication, Reporting, and Conformance) combines SPF and DKIM to provide an additional layer of protection. Implementing these protocols helps prevent spoofing and improves your email deliverability.

Regularly cleaning your email list is essential for maintaining a strong sender reputation. Over time, email lists can accumulate invalid addresses, inactive subscribers, and spam traps. Removing these addresses from your list helps improve your deliverability rates and engagement metrics. Use tools and strategies like double opt-in, list verification services, and engagement-based segmentation to keep your email list clean and healthy.

Avoiding purchased email lists is crucial. While it might be tempting to buy a list of email addresses to quickly grow your audience, these lists often contain invalid addresses, spam traps, and recipients who haven't consented to receive your emails. Sending to these addresses can harm your sender reputation and increase the likelihood of your emails being marked as spam. Focus on building an organic email list through legitimate means like website sign-ups and social media campaigns.

Building an organic email list involves collecting email addresses from people who have actively shown interest in your content or products. This can be done through sign-up forms on your website, social media promotions, and in-person events. Offering incentives like discounts, free resources, or exclusive content can encourage sign-ups. An organic list is more likely to engage with your emails, improving your sender reputation and overall email marketing success.

The content of your emails plays a significant role in your sender reputation. Emails that are relevant, engaging, and valuable to your audience are more likely to be opened and less likely to be marked as spam. Focus on creating content that addresses your audience's needs and interests. Personalize your messages, use clear and compelling subject lines, and include a strong call-to-action to encourage engagement.

Personalization and relevance are key to email success. Personalizing your emails with the recipient's name, past purchase behavior, and other relevant information makes your messages feel more tailored and engaging. This not only improves your engagement rates but also builds trust with your audience. Relevant content that addresses your audience's interests and needs is more likely to be opened and acted upon.

Writing engaging subject lines is an art. A good subject line grabs the recipient's attention and entices them to open the email. It should be clear, concise, and relevant to the content of the email. Avoid using all caps, excessive punctuation, and spammy words. Instead, focus on creating curiosity, offering value, and personalizing the subject line to the recipient's interests.

A/B testing is a powerful tool for improving your sender reputation. By testing different elements of your emails, such as subject lines, content, and call-to-actions, you can identify what resonates with your audience and improve your engagement rates. Regularly conducting A/B tests helps you stay ahead of trends and continuously optimize your email marketing strategy.

Monitoring your sender reputation involves regularly checking key metrics like open rates, click-through rates, bounce rates, and spam complaints. Use tools and services that provide insights into your reputation and deliverability. By keeping a close eye on these metrics, you can identify and address any issues early, ensuring your emails continue to reach your audience's inboxes.

Managing your sender reputation requires a proactive approach. Regularly clean your email list, send relevant and engaging content, and monitor your reputation metrics. Use authentication protocols to protect your emails and avoid practices that can harm your reputation, like using purchased lists or sending too many emails. By following these best practices, you can build and maintain a strong sender reputation.

Common mistakes to avoid include sending irrelevant content, neglecting email list hygiene, and failing to authenticate your emails. These practices can harm your sender reputation and increase the likelihood of your emails being marked as spam. By understanding and avoiding these mistakes, you can improve your email deliverability and build a stronger relationship with your audience.

Now that we've covered the importance of building a strong sender reputation, let's move on to crafting spam-free content. This chapter will guide you through the elements of creating emails that not only engage your audience but also stay out of the spam folder.

Chapter 3: Crafting Spam-Free Content

———

Crafting spam-free content is like preparing a delicious meal; it requires the right ingredients, careful preparation, and attention to detail. The components of email content include the subject line, preheader, body text, images, and call-to-action. Each element plays a crucial role in determining whether your email gets delivered to the inbox or ends up in the spam folder. Understanding how to create compelling and relevant content can help you avoid spam filters and engage your audience effectively.

The subject line is the first thing recipients see, and it can make or break your email's success. A good subject line grabs attention, creates curiosity, and entices the recipient to open the email. It should be clear, concise, and relevant to the content of the email. Avoid using all caps, excessive punctuation, and spammy words like "free" and "urgent." Instead, focus on creating curiosity, offering value, and personalizing the subject line to the recipient's interests.

Email preheaders are the next thing recipients see, and they provide additional context to the subject line. A well-written preheader can increase open rates by providing a sneak peek of the email's content. It should complement the subject line and give recipients a reason to open the email. Keep it concise, relevant, and engaging to maximize its impact.

The body of the email is where you deliver your message. It should be clear, concise, and easy to read. Use short paragraphs, bullet points, and headings to break up the text and make it more scannable. Focus on providing value to the recipient, whether it's information, a special offer, or a call-to-action. Avoid using excessive links, images, and attachments, as these can trigger spam filters.

Images and videos can enhance your emails and make them more engaging. However, they can also increase the likelihood of your emails being marked as spam if not used correctly. Use images sparingly and ensure they are relevant to the content. Include alt text for each image to provide context for recipients who have images disabled. Videos should be embedded or linked appropriately to avoid large file sizes.

HTML vs. plain text emails is a common debate among email marketers. HTML emails allow for more design options and visual appeal, but they can also be flagged as spam more easily. Plain text emails, on the other hand, are simpler and less likely to be marked as spam but may not be as visually engaging. Finding the right balance between the two can help you create effective and spam-free emails.

Balancing text and visual content is crucial for keeping your emails out of the spam folder. Too many images or links can trigger spam filters, while too much text can make your emails less engaging. Aim for a mix of both, ensuring your content is relevant, concise, and easy to read. This balance helps create a positive user experience and improves your email deliverability.

Writing a compelling call-to-action (CTA) is essential for encouraging recipients to take the desired action. Whether it's clicking a link, making a purchase, or signing up for a webinar, your CTA should be clear, concise, and compelling. Use action-oriented language and create a sense of urgency to motivate recipients to act. Avoid using spammy words like "buy now" and "limited time offer," as these can trigger spam filters.

Personalization is key to creating engaging and spam-free emails. By using the recipient's name, past purchase behavior, and other relevant information, you can make your emails feel more tailored and relevant. Personalization not only improves engagement rates but also reduces the likelihood of your emails being marked as spam. Use dynamic content and merge tags to personalize your emails effectively.

Dynamic content allows you to tailor different parts of your email to different segments of your audience. This can include personalized greetings, product recommendations, and targeted offers. By creating more relevant and engaging content, you can improve your email deliverability and build stronger connections with your audience.

Real-life examples of effective email content provide valuable insights into what works and what doesn't. For instance, a company that used personalized subject lines and dynamic content saw a significant increase in their open and click-through rates. These examples highlight the importance of understanding your audience and continuously optimizing your email content to meet their needs.

Storytelling is a powerful tool in email marketing. By telling a compelling story, you can capture your audience's attention and keep them engaged. Whether it's sharing a customer success story, explaining the journey of your product, or describing how your service can solve a problem, storytelling helps create a connection with your audience and makes your emails more memorable.

Humor can also be an effective way to engage your audience and make your emails stand out. A well-placed joke or light-hearted comment can create a positive impression and make your emails more enjoyable to read. However, it's important to use humor appropriately and ensure it aligns with your brand voice and audience preferences.

Readability is crucial for keeping your audience engaged. Use short paragraphs, bullet points, and headings to break up the text and make it more scannable. Choose fonts and colors that are easy to read, and avoid using too many different fonts and styles. Ensuring your emails are easy to read helps create a positive user experience and reduces the likelihood of your emails being marked as spam.

Mobile optimization is essential in today's digital world, where many people read emails on their smartphones. Ensure your emails are responsive and look good on all devices by using a mobile-friendly design. Test your emails on different devices and screen sizes to ensure they are easy to read and navigate, regardless of how they are accessed.

Testing your emails across devices and platforms is crucial for ensuring they display correctly and don't trigger spam filters. Use tools that simulate how your emails will look on different devices and email clients. Regularly testing your emails helps you catch and fix any issues before they impact your email deliverability and engagement rates.

Common content mistakes to avoid include using spammy words, sending irrelevant content, and neglecting personalization. These practices can harm your sender reputation and increase the likelihood of your emails being marked as spam. By understanding and avoiding these mistakes, you can improve your email deliverability and create more engaging content.

Using email templates effectively can save you time and ensure consistency in your emails. Choose templates that are responsive, easy to customize, and aligned with your brand. Regularly update your templates to reflect changes in your content and design strategy. Templates help streamline your email creation process and maintain a consistent look and feel across your campaigns.

Crafting spam-free content is an ongoing process that requires continuous learning and optimization. By staying informed about best practices, regularly testing your emails, and focusing on creating relevant and engaging content, you can improve your email deliverability and build stronger connections with your audience.

As we move forward, it's important to consider how to manage and segment your email list effectively. The next chapter will guide you through the best practices for email list management and segmentation, helping you create targeted and personalized email campaigns that resonate with your audience.

Chapter 4: Email List Management and Segmentation

———

Email list management is like tending a garden. Just as a garden needs regular care and attention to thrive, your email list requires ongoing maintenance to ensure it remains healthy and effective. This involves building a high-quality email list, regularly cleaning it, and using segmentation to target your audience more effectively. Proper list management helps improve your email deliverability, engagement rates, and overall marketing success.

Building a high-quality email list starts with collecting email addresses from people who have shown genuine interest in your content or products. This can be done through sign-up forms on your website, social media campaigns, and in-person events. Offering incentives like discounts, free resources, or exclusive content can encourage sign-ups. A high-quality list is more likely to engage with your emails and less likely to mark them as spam.

Growing your email list involves continuously finding new ways to attract subscribers. This can include running social media promotions, collaborating with influencers, and creating valuable content that encourages sign-ups. Focus on attracting subscribers who are genuinely interested in your content and products, as they are more likely to engage with your emails and less likely to mark them as spam.

Segmenting your email list involves dividing it into smaller groups based on specific criteria, such as demographics, behavior, or interests. This allows you to send more targeted and personalized emails, which can improve your engagement rates and deliverability. Segmentation helps ensure your emails are relevant to each recipient, reducing the likelihood of them being marked as spam.

The benefits of email list segmentation are numerous. By sending targeted emails, you can improve your open and click-through rates, increase conversions, and build stronger relationships with your audience. Segmentation also helps reduce unsubscribe rates and spam complaints, as recipients are more likely to find your emails relevant and valuable.

There are many ways to segment your email list, including demographic information (age, gender, location), behavioral data (purchase history, browsing behavior), and engagement metrics (open rates, click-through rates). The key is to find the criteria that are most relevant to your business and audience. Experiment with different segmentation strategies to see what works best for you.

Successful segmentation often involves using data to create customer personas. These personas represent different segments of your audience and help you understand their needs, preferences, and behaviors. By tailoring your email content to these personas, you can create more relevant and engaging emails that resonate with your audience.

Effective email targeting involves understanding your audience and using data to send the right message to the right person at the right time. This means using segmentation to identify different audience groups and creating personalized content for each group. By targeting your emails more effectively, you can improve your engagement rates and overall email marketing success.

Creating personalized email campaigns involves using the data you have about your subscribers to tailor your messages to their interests and needs. This can include using their name, past purchase behavior, and other relevant information to make your emails feel more personal and relevant. Personalization not only improves engagement rates but also builds trust and loyalty with your audience.

Segmentation can significantly impact email engagement by ensuring your emails are relevant to each recipient. When your emails address the specific needs and interests of your audience, they are more likely to be opened, read, and acted upon. This not only improves your engagement metrics but also enhances your sender reputation and overall email deliverability.

There are many tools available for managing your email lists and implementing segmentation. These tools can help you collect and analyze data, create segments, and automate personalized email campaigns. Using the right tools can streamline your list management process and ensure you are sending the most relevant and engaging emails to your audience.

Handling unsubscribes effectively is an important part of email list management. Make it easy for recipients to unsubscribe if they no longer want to receive your emails. This helps reduce spam complaints and maintain a positive sender reputation. Providing a simple and clear unsubscribe process shows respect for your audience's preferences and can improve their overall experience with your brand.

Re-engagement campaigns are a valuable strategy for reconnecting with inactive subscribers. These campaigns can include special offers, personalized content, or a simple reminder of the value you provide. By re-engaging inactive subscribers, you can improve your engagement metrics and make the most of your existing email list.

Avoiding email list fatigue involves finding the right balance in your sending frequency. Sending too many emails can overwhelm your subscribers and lead to unsubscribes and spam complaints. On the other hand, sending too few emails can cause your audience to forget about you. Test different frequencies to find the sweet spot that keeps your audience engaged without overwhelming them.

The frequency of your email campaigns can have a significant impact on your engagement rates. Finding the right frequency involves testing different schedules and monitoring your engagement metrics. Pay attention to how your audience responds to different frequencies and adjust your strategy accordingly. Consistency is key, but be flexible and willing to make changes based on your data.

Testing email frequency involves experimenting with different sending schedules and analyzing the results. Use A/B testing to compare the performance of different frequencies and identify what works best for your audience. Regular testing helps you stay agile and responsive to changes in your audience's preferences and behaviors.

The timing of your emails can also impact engagement. Sending your emails at the right time can increase the likelihood that they will be opened and read.

Consider factors like your audience's time zone, daily routines, and typical email habits when deciding on the best send times. Test different times to see what works best for your audience.

Determining the best send times involves analyzing your engagement metrics and testing different schedules. Use tools that provide insights into when your audience is most likely to open and interact with your emails. By finding the optimal send times, you can improve your open and click-through rates and make the most of your email marketing efforts.

Scheduling your emails effectively ensures they reach your audience at the right time. Use email marketing tools that allow you to schedule your emails in advance and send them at the optimal times. This helps you stay organized and ensures your emails are delivered when your audience is most likely to engage with them.

Common email list management mistakes include neglecting list hygiene, sending irrelevant content, and failing to segment your audience. These practices can harm your sender reputation and reduce your engagement rates. By understanding and avoiding these mistakes, you can improve your email deliverability and create more effective email campaigns.

Proper email list management is an ongoing process that requires continuous attention and optimization. By regularly cleaning your list, segmenting your audience, and sending relevant and personalized emails, you can improve your email deliverability and engagement rates. Stay informed about best practices and use the right tools to manage your list effectively.

Now that we've covered the importance of email list management and segmentation, it's time to explore how to ensure compliance with email laws. The next chapter will guide you through the key requirements of major email marketing laws and how to stay compliant, protecting your sender reputation and avoiding legal issues.

Chapter 5: Ensuring Compliance with Email Laws

Email marketing laws are like the rules of the road for digital communication. They set the standards for how you can collect, use, and share email addresses, protecting recipients from unwanted emails and ensuring fair practices. Understanding and complying with these laws is crucial for maintaining a positive sender reputation and avoiding legal issues. This chapter will guide you through the key requirements of major email marketing laws and how to stay compliant.

Compliance is not just about avoiding fines and penalties; it's also about building trust with your audience. When you follow the rules, you show your subscribers that you respect their privacy and preferences. This can improve your engagement rates and help you build a loyal audience. By staying compliant, you protect your sender reputation and enhance the effectiveness of your email marketing efforts.

The CAN-SPAM Act is one of the most well-known email marketing laws in the United States. It sets the standards for commercial emails, requiring that they include accurate subject lines, clear identification as an advertisement, a valid physical address, and an easy way to opt-out. Violating the CAN-SPAM Act can result in hefty fines, so it's important to understand and follow its requirements.

Key requirements of the CAN-SPAM Act include providing a clear and conspicuous way for recipients to opt-out of receiving future emails. This can be done through an unsubscribe link or a similar mechanism. You must also honor opt-out requests promptly, within 10 business days. Additionally, your emails must include your valid physical postal address and a clear identification that the message is an advertisement.

Compliance with the CAN-SPAM Act involves regularly reviewing and updating your email practices to ensure they meet the law's requirements. This includes regularly testing your opt-out mechanisms, verifying the accuracy of your email content, and ensuring your physical address is up-to-date. By staying on top of these requirements, you can avoid legal issues and build trust with your audience.

The GDPR (General Data Protection Regulation) is another important email marketing law, particularly for businesses operating in the European Union. The GDPR sets strict rules for collecting, using, and storing personal data, including email addresses. It requires that you obtain explicit consent from individuals before sending them marketing emails and that you provide clear and transparent information about how their data will be used.

Key requirements of the GDPR include obtaining explicit consent from subscribers before adding them to your email list. This means they must actively agree to receive your emails, usually by checking a box or clicking a confirmation link. You must also provide clear and transparent information about how their data will be used, including your privacy policy and any third parties that may have access to their data.

Compliance with the GDPR involves implementing practices that ensure you obtain and manage consent properly. This includes using double opt-in for email sign-ups, regularly reviewing and updating your privacy policy, and ensuring your data storage and processing practices meet the GDPR's requirements. By staying compliant, you can protect your business from hefty fines and build trust with your European audience.

The impact of email laws on marketing is significant. Non-compliance can result in fines, legal action, and damage to your sender reputation. It can also erode trust with your audience, leading to lower engagement rates and higher unsubscribe rates. By understanding and following email laws, you can protect your business, build trust with your audience, and improve your email marketing success.

Real-life examples of non-compliance highlight the importance of following email laws. For instance, a company that failed to honor opt-out requests faced significant fines and legal action. These examples underscore the importance of understanding and complying with the requirements of email laws to protect your business and maintain a positive sender reputation.

Consent is a fundamental aspect of email marketing compliance. It ensures that recipients have agreed to receive your emails and are more likely to engage with them. Obtaining explicit consent involves using clear and transparent sign-up forms, providing detailed information about how their data will be used, and ensuring they have actively agreed to receive your emails.

Creating compliant sign-up forms is essential for obtaining explicit consent. Your forms should be clear and transparent, providing detailed information about what subscribers can expect to receive and how their data will be used. Use double opt-in to confirm their consent and provide a clear and easy way for them to opt-out if they change their mind.

A privacy policy is a critical component of email marketing compliance. It provides detailed information about how you collect, use, and store personal data, including email addresses. Your privacy policy should be clear and transparent, explaining how you will use subscribers' data, who will have access to it, and how they can contact you with questions or concerns.

Creating a clear privacy policy involves regularly reviewing and updating it to reflect any changes in your data collection and processing practices. Make sure your privacy policy is easily accessible on your website and in your email sign-up forms. Providing a clear and transparent privacy policy helps build trust with your audience and ensures compliance with email laws.

Unsubscribe mechanisms are essential for compliance with email marketing laws. They provide recipients with a clear and easy way to opt-out of receiving future emails. Your unsubscribe link should be prominently displayed in your emails, and opt-out requests should be honored promptly. By providing a simple and clear unsubscribe process, you can reduce spam complaints and maintain a positive sender reputation.

Transparency is key to compliance with email marketing laws. Be clear and honest with your subscribers about what they can expect to receive, how their data will be used, and how they can opt-out if they choose. Providing transparent information helps build trust with your audience and ensures compliance with email laws.

Handling data breaches responsibly is crucial for compliance and maintaining trust with your audience. If you experience a data breach, notify affected individuals promptly and provide clear information about what happened, what data was affected, and what steps you are taking to address the issue. By handling data breaches responsibly, you can protect your reputation and comply with legal requirements.

International email laws vary, so it's important to understand the requirements in the countries where your subscribers are located. Research the email marketing laws in different regions and ensure your practices comply with them. This helps you avoid legal issues and build trust with your international audience.

Staying updated on email laws involves regularly reviewing legal resources, participating in industry forums, and consulting with legal experts. Email marketing laws are constantly evolving, so it's important to stay informed about changes and updates. By staying updated, you can ensure your practices remain compliant and protect your business from legal issues.

Tools for ensuring compliance can help you manage consent, monitor your email practices, and stay informed about legal requirements. Use tools that provide insights into your compliance status, automate consent management, and help you monitor your email deliverability and engagement metrics. By using the right tools, you can streamline your compliance efforts and protect your sender reputation.

Common compliance mistakes include failing to obtain explicit consent, neglecting unsubscribe requests, and not providing clear and transparent information about data usage. These practices can lead to legal issues and damage your sender reputation. By understanding and avoiding these mistakes, you can improve your compliance efforts and build trust with your audience.

Successful compliance involves a combination of clear communication, regular monitoring, and continuous improvement. By providing transparent information, regularly reviewing your practices, and staying informed about legal requirements, you can ensure compliance and build trust with your audience. Stay proactive and responsive to changes in email marketing laws to protect your business and enhance your email marketing success.

Now that we've explored how to ensure compliance with email laws, it's time to delve into the technical aspects of email marketing. The next chapter will guide you through leveraging email authentication and security to protect your emails and improve your deliverability.

Chapter 6: Leveraging Email Authentication and Security

———

Email authentication and security are like the locks and keys that protect your emails from unauthorized access and ensure they reach their intended recipients. Authentication protocols verify that your emails come from a legitimate source, while security measures protect your emails and data from threats like phishing and spoofing. Understanding and implementing these technologies is crucial for improving your email deliverability and maintaining a positive sender reputation.

Email authentication is a set of protocols that verify the sender's identity and ensure the email has not been tampered with during transit. The most common authentication protocols are SPF (Sender Policy Framework), DKIM (DomainKeys Identified Mail), and DMARC (Domain-based Message Authentication, Reporting, and Conformance). These protocols work together to protect your emails and improve your deliverability.

SPF (Sender Policy Framework) is an email authentication protocol that verifies the sending server's IP address. It allows the domain owner to specify which servers are authorized to send emails on their behalf. Implementing SPF helps prevent spoofing and improves your email deliverability by ensuring your emails come from a trusted source.

Implementing SPF involves creating a TXT record in your domain's DNS settings. This record lists the IP addresses of the servers authorized to send emails on behalf of your domain. By doing this, you help email providers verify that your emails are legitimate and not sent by spammers pretending to be you.

DKIM (DomainKeys Identified Mail) adds a digital signature to your emails, ensuring they have not been altered during transit. This signature is generated using a private key and verified by the recipient's email provider using a public key published in your domain's DNS settings. Implementing DKIM helps protect your emails from tampering and improves your email deliverability.

To implement DKIM, you need to generate a pair of cryptographic keys (one private and one public) and publish the public key in your domain's DNS settings. The private key is used to sign your emails, and the recipient's email provider verifies the signature using the public key. This ensures that your emails have not been altered and come from a trusted source.

DMARC (Domain-based Message Authentication, Reporting, and Conformance) builds on SPF and DKIM to provide an additional layer of protection. It allows domain owners to specify how email providers should handle emails that fail SPF or DKIM checks. DMARC also provides detailed reports on email authentication activity, helping you monitor and improve your email security.

Implementing DMARC involves creating a TXT record in your domain's DNS settings that specifies your DMARC policy. This policy can instruct email providers to quarantine, reject, or allow emails that fail SPF or DKIM checks. By implementing DMARC, you can protect your domain from spoofing and improve your email deliverability.

Monitoring email authentication involves regularly reviewing your SPF, DKIM, and DMARC settings and ensuring they are correctly configured. Use tools that provide insights into your email authentication status and alert you to any issues. Regular monitoring helps you maintain a high level of email security and deliverability.

Email encryption is another important aspect of email security. Encryption protects the content of your emails from being intercepted and read by unauthorized parties. There are different types of email encryption, including end-to-end encryption and transport layer security (TLS). Implementing encryption helps protect your sensitive data and build trust with your audience.

Implementing email encryption involves configuring your email server to use TLS for sending and receiving emails. This ensures that your emails are encrypted during transit, protecting them from interception. End-to-end encryption provides an additional layer of protection by encrypting the email content itself, ensuring only the intended recipient can read it.

Securing email data involves implementing best practices for data protection, such as using strong passwords, regularly updating your security software, and monitoring for suspicious activity. Protecting your email data helps prevent breaches and unauthorized access, building trust with your audience and protecting your sender reputation.

Phishing and spoofing are common threats to email security. Phishing involves sending emails that appear to come from a trusted source but contain malicious links or attachments. Spoofing involves forging the sender's email address to make it look like the email comes from someone else. Understanding these threats and implementing measures to prevent them is crucial for email security.

Preventing phishing attacks involves educating your audience about the risks and how to recognize phishing emails. Use clear and transparent communication, and include security tips in your emails. Implementing email authentication protocols like SPF, DKIM, and DMARC also helps prevent phishing by verifying the sender's identity.

Detecting and responding to spoofing involves monitoring your email activity for signs of unauthorized access and taking action to address any issues. Use tools that provide insights into your email authentication status and alert you to potential spoofing attempts. Respond promptly to any signs of spoofing to protect your domain and maintain your sender reputation.

Email security protocols like SPF, DKIM, and DMARC play a crucial role in protecting your emails and improving your deliverability. Regularly review and update your security settings to ensure they are correctly configured and effective. By implementing these protocols, you can protect your emails from unauthorized access and improve your email marketing success.

Staying updated on email security involves regularly reviewing industry resources, participating in forums, and consulting with security experts. Email security threats are constantly evolving, so it's important to stay informed about new risks and best practices. By staying updated, you can ensure your email security measures remain effective and protect your business from threats.

Real-life stories of email security breaches highlight the importance of implementing strong security measures. For instance, a company that failed to implement email encryption experienced a data breach that compromised sensitive customer information. These examples underscore the importance of understanding and implementing email security best practices to protect your business and build trust with your audience.

Best practices for email security include using strong passwords, regularly updating your security software, implementing email authentication protocols, and educating your audience about security risks. By following these best practices, you can protect your emails from threats and improve your email deliverability and engagement rates.

Common email security mistakes include failing to implement email authentication protocols, neglecting to encrypt sensitive data, and not monitoring for suspicious activity. These practices can leave your emails vulnerable to threats and harm your sender reputation. By understanding and avoiding these mistakes, you can improve your email security and protect your business.

Now that we've covered the importance of email authentication and security, it's time to focus on monitoring and analyzing your email performance. The next chapter will guide you through the key metrics to track and how to use data to improve your email campaigns.

Chapter 7: Monitoring and Analyzing Email Performance

———

Monitoring and analyzing email performance is like keeping a pulse on your email marketing health. It involves tracking key metrics, understanding what they mean, and using the data to make informed decisions. By regularly monitoring your performance, you can identify areas for improvement, optimize your campaigns, and achieve better results. This chapter will guide you through the key metrics to track and how to use data to improve your email marketing success.

Email performance monitoring involves tracking various metrics, such as open rates, click-through rates, bounce rates, and spam complaints. Each of these metrics provides insights into different aspects of your email campaigns, helping you understand how well your emails are performing and where improvements are needed. Regularly monitoring these metrics helps you stay informed about your email performance and make data-driven decisions.

Open rates are one of the most important metrics to track. They indicate how many recipients opened your emails and can give you insights into the effectiveness of your subject lines and preheaders. High open rates suggest that your emails are capturing your audience's attention, while low open rates may indicate that your subject lines need improvement.

Click-through rates (CTR) measure how many recipients clicked on links within your emails. This metric indicates the level of engagement with your email content and the effectiveness of your call-to-actions. High CTRs suggest that your content is relevant and compelling, while low CTRs may indicate that your content needs to be more engaging or that your CTAs need improvement.

Bounce rates measure the percentage of emails that were not delivered to recipients. There are two types of bounces: hard bounces and soft bounces. Hard bounces occur when the email address is invalid or does not exist, while soft bounces occur when the recipient's mailbox is full or the server is temporarily unavailable. High bounce rates can harm your sender reputation, so it's important to regularly clean your email list to remove invalid addresses.

Reducing bounce rates involves regularly cleaning your email list, using double opt-in to verify email addresses, and monitoring your bounce rate metrics. By keeping your email list clean and up-to-date, you can improve your deliverability and reduce the likelihood of your emails bouncing.

Delivery rates indicate the percentage of emails that were successfully delivered to recipients. High delivery rates suggest that your emails are reaching your audience, while low delivery rates may indicate issues with your sender reputation or email list quality. Monitoring your delivery rates helps you identify and address any issues that may be affecting your email deliverability.

Tracking email deliverability involves using tools that provide insights into your delivery rates, bounce rates, and other relevant metrics. Regularly monitoring these metrics helps you stay informed about your email performance and identify any issues that need addressing. By tracking your deliverability, you can ensure your emails are reaching your audience and achieving your marketing goals.

Email engagement metrics, such as open rates, click-through rates, and conversion rates, provide insights into how well your emails are resonating with your audience. High engagement metrics suggest that your content is relevant and compelling, while low engagement metrics may indicate that your content needs improvement. Regularly monitoring these metrics helps you optimize your email campaigns for better results.

A/B testing is a powerful tool for improving your email performance. By testing different elements of your emails, such as subject lines, content, and call-to-actions, you can identify what resonates with your audience and optimize your campaigns accordingly. Regularly conducting A/B tests helps you stay ahead of trends and continuously improve your email marketing strategy.

Setting up A/B tests involves creating two or more versions of your email and sending them to different segments of your audience. By comparing the performance of each version, you can identify which elements are most effective and make data-driven decisions to optimize your campaigns. A/B testing helps you understand what works best for your audience and improve your email performance.

Interpreting A/B test results involves analyzing the data to identify trends and patterns. Look at metrics such as open rates, click-through rates, and conversion rates to determine which version of your email performed best. Use these insights to make informed decisions about future email campaigns and continuously improve your email marketing strategy.

Email analytics provide valuable insights into your email performance. Use tools that offer detailed analytics and reporting to track key metrics, monitor your campaigns, and identify areas for improvement. By leveraging email analytics, you can make data-driven decisions to optimize your email marketing efforts and achieve better results.

Creating email performance reports involves compiling data from your email analytics and presenting it in a clear and actionable format. Include key metrics such as open rates, click-through rates, bounce rates, and conversion rates, along with insights and recommendations for improvement. Regularly reviewing and sharing these reports helps you stay informed about your email performance and make data-driven decisions.

Using data to improve your email campaigns involves analyzing your performance metrics, identifying trends and patterns, and making informed decisions to optimize your strategy. Look for areas where your performance is strong and replicate those successes, while also identifying areas for improvement and making necessary adjustments. By leveraging data, you can continuously improve your email marketing efforts and achieve better results.

Segmentation plays a significant role in email performance. By dividing your email list into smaller, targeted segments, you can send more relevant and personalized emails, which can improve your engagement rates and overall performance. Use data to identify different segments of your audience and tailor your email content to their specific needs and interests.

Tracking segmentation success involves monitoring the performance of different segments of your email list. Look at metrics such as open rates, click-through rates, and conversion rates for each segment to determine how well your segmentation strategy is working. Use these insights to refine your segmentation and improve your email performance.

Personalization is key to improving email performance. By using data to personalize your emails with the recipient's name, past purchase behavior, and other relevant information, you can create more engaging and relevant content. Personalization not only improves engagement rates but also builds trust and loyalty with your audience.

Measuring the ROI of email marketing involves tracking the revenue generated from your email campaigns and comparing it to the costs of running those campaigns. Look at metrics such as conversion rates, average order value, and customer lifetime value to determine the financial impact of your email marketing efforts. By measuring ROI, you can assess the effectiveness of your email campaigns and make informed decisions to optimize your strategy.

Common performance monitoring mistakes include neglecting to track key metrics, failing to regularly review and analyze data, and not using data to make informed decisions. These practices can hinder your email marketing success and prevent you from achieving your goals. By understanding and avoiding these mistakes, you can improve your performance monitoring efforts and achieve better results.

Now that we've covered the importance of monitoring and analyzing email performance, it's time to explore how to optimize your email design for deliverability. The next chapter will guide you through best practices for email design, helping you create visually appealing and engaging emails that reach your audience's inboxes.

Chapter 8: Optimizing Email Design for Deliverability

Optimizing email design for deliverability is like creating a visually appealing and functional masterpiece. Your email design not only needs to look good but also needs to ensure it reaches your audience's inboxes and engages them effectively. This chapter will guide you through best practices for email design, helping you create visually appealing and engaging emails that improve your deliverability and overall email marketing success.

The importance of email design cannot be overstated. A well-designed email captures your audience's attention, provides a positive user experience, and encourages engagement. It also helps improve your email deliverability by ensuring your emails are easy to read, visually appealing, and compliant with email best practices. By focusing on design, you can create emails that stand out and achieve better results.

Email design impacts deliverability in several ways. For instance, emails with too many images or large file sizes can trigger spam filters. Similarly, emails that are not mobile-friendly or difficult to read can lead to higher bounce rates and lower engagement. By optimizing your design, you can improve your email deliverability and ensure your messages reach your audience's inboxes.

Designing spam-free emails involves using best practices that reduce the likelihood of your emails being marked as spam. This includes using a balanced mix of text and images, avoiding excessive links and attachments, and ensuring your content is relevant and engaging. By following these best practices, you can create visually appealing emails that stay out of the spam folder.

Responsive design is crucial for ensuring your emails look good on all devices. With many people reading emails on their smartphones, it's essential to create emails that are mobile-friendly and responsive. Use a responsive email template that automatically adjusts to different screen sizes and test your emails on various devices to ensure they display correctly.

Creating mobile-friendly emails involves using a single-column layout, larger fonts, and clear call-to-actions. Avoid using small text or too many images, as these can be difficult to read on mobile devices. Ensure your links and buttons are easy to click, and test your emails on different devices to ensure they are easy to navigate and read.

Images can enhance your emails and make them more engaging, but they can also impact your deliverability if not used correctly. Use images sparingly and ensure they are relevant to the content. Include alt text for each image to provide context for recipients who have images disabled. Optimize your images to reduce file sizes and ensure your emails load quickly.

Using alt text in email design is important for accessibility and deliverability. Alt text provides a description of the image for recipients who have images disabled or use screen readers. This helps ensure your emails are accessible to all recipients and improves your deliverability by providing context for your images.

Colors play a significant role in email design. They can evoke emotions, create a sense of urgency, and enhance your brand identity. Use colors that align with your brand and create a visually appealing design. Avoid using too many different colors, as this can make your emails look cluttered and unprofessional.

Fonts impact readability and overall design. Choose fonts that are easy to read and align with your brand identity. Avoid using too many different fonts or styles, as this can make your emails look cluttered and unprofessional. Use a font size that is easy to read on all devices, and test your emails to ensure they are readable.

Structuring your email layout is crucial for creating a visually appealing and engaging design. Use a clear and logical layout that guides the recipient's eye through the content. Include headings, subheadings, and bullet points to break up the text and make it more scannable. Ensure your call-to-actions are prominently displayed and easy to find.

White space is an important element of email design. It helps create a clean and uncluttered look, making your content easier to read and navigate. Use white space to separate different sections of your email and highlight important elements. This not only improves readability but also enhances the overall visual appeal of your emails.

Creating clear call-to-actions (CTAs) is essential for encouraging recipients to take the desired action. Your CTAs should be prominently displayed, easy to understand, and action-oriented. Use contrasting colors and clear language to make your CTAs stand out. Test different CTAs to see what resonates best with your audience.

Buttons are an effective way to create visually appealing and clickable CTAs. Use buttons instead of text links to make your CTAs more noticeable and easier to click. Ensure your buttons are large enough to be easily tapped on mobile devices and use clear and compelling language to encourage action.

Email width impacts deliverability and readability. Use a width of 600-800 pixels to ensure your emails display correctly on most devices and email clients. This width is optimal for creating a balanced and visually appealing design that is easy to read and navigate.

Setting the right email width involves using a responsive template and testing your emails on different devices and email clients. Ensure your emails are easy to read and navigate, regardless of the device or screen size. By setting the right width, you can create a positive user experience and improve your email deliverability.

Designing accessible emails is crucial for ensuring all recipients can read and engage with your content. Use clear and concise language, descriptive alt text for images, and a logical layout. Avoid using color alone to convey important information and ensure your emails are compatible with screen readers.

Email load times impact deliverability and user experience. Emails that take too long to load can lead to higher bounce rates and lower engagement. Optimize your images, minimize the use of large files and scripts, and use a responsive design to ensure your emails load quickly on all devices.

Reducing email load times involves optimizing your images, using compressed file formats, and minimizing the use of large files and scripts. Test your emails to ensure they load quickly on different devices and email clients. By reducing load times, you can improve your email deliverability and user experience.

Testing your email designs is essential for ensuring they display correctly and don't trigger spam filters. Use tools that simulate how your emails will look on different devices and email clients. Regularly testing your emails helps you catch and fix any issues before they impact your email deliverability and engagement rates.

Common design mistakes to avoid include using too many images, neglecting mobile optimization, and failing to test your emails. These practices can harm your sender reputation and reduce your engagement rates. By understanding and avoiding these mistakes, you can create visually appealing and effective email designs that improve your deliverability and overall email marketing success.

Using email templates effectively can save you time and ensure consistency in your designs. Choose templates that are responsive, easy to customize, and aligned with your brand. Regularly update your templates to reflect changes in your content and design strategy. Templates help streamline your email creation process and maintain a consistent look and feel across your campaigns.

Now that we've covered the importance of optimizing email design for deliverability, it's time to focus on engaging your audience with compelling content. The next chapter will guide you through best practices for creating engaging and relevant content that resonates with your audience and improves your email marketing success.

Chapter 9: Engaging Your Audience with Content

———

Engaging your audience with compelling content is like telling a captivating story. It captures their attention, keeps them interested, and encourages them to take action. Creating engaging content involves understanding your audience, using storytelling techniques, and personalizing your messages. This chapter will guide you through best practices for creating engaging and relevant content that resonates with your audience and improves your email marketing success.

Understanding your audience is the first step in creating engaging content. Know their interests, preferences, and pain points. Use data and insights to create content that addresses their needs and provides value. When you understand your audience, you can create content that resonates with them and encourages engagement.

Audience engagement is crucial for email marketing success. Engaged recipients are more likely to open, read, and act on your emails. This not only improves your engagement metrics but also enhances your sender reputation and deliverability. Focus on creating content that is relevant, valuable, and interesting to your audience.

Creating engaging content involves using storytelling techniques to capture your audience's attention. Tell a compelling story that resonates with your audience and makes your emails more memorable. Whether it's sharing a customer success story, explaining the journey of your product, or describing how your service can solve a problem, storytelling helps create a connection with your audience.

Storytelling can be a powerful tool in email marketing. It makes your emails more interesting and relatable, creating an emotional connection with your audience. Use storytelling to illustrate your points, share experiences, and convey your message in a way that engages and inspires your audience.

Writing for your audience involves using a tone and voice that resonates with them. Whether it's casual and friendly or professional and authoritative, your tone should reflect your brand and appeal to your audience. Use clear and concise language, and avoid jargon or complex terms that might confuse your readers.

The tone and voice of your emails can significantly impact engagement. Find the right balance that reflects your brand and appeals to your audience. Test different tones and voices to see what resonates best, and use feedback to refine your approach. By finding the right tone, you can create more engaging and relatable content.

Using humor in your emails can make them more enjoyable and memorable. A well-placed joke or light-hearted comment can create a positive impression and make your emails stand out. However, it's important to use humor appropriately and ensure it aligns with your brand voice and audience preferences.

Humor can be a double-edged sword, so use it carefully. What one person finds funny, another might find offensive. Test your humorous content with a small segment of your audience before rolling it out to your entire list. If used correctly, humor can make your emails more engaging and build a stronger connection with your audience.

Emotions play a significant role in engagement. Evoke emotions through your content to create a deeper connection with your audience. Whether it's excitement, curiosity, or empathy, emotions can make your emails more impactful and memorable. Use storytelling, imagery, and language to evoke the right emotions.

Relevance is key to creating engaging content. Ensure your emails are relevant to your audience's interests and needs. Use data and insights to tailor your content and provide value. When your content is relevant, your audience is more likely to engage with it and take the desired action.

Making content relevant involves using personalization and segmentation to tailor your messages to different audience groups. Use data like past purchase behavior, browsing history, and demographic information to create personalized content that resonates with each segment. Personalization not only improves engagement rates but also builds trust and loyalty with your audience.

Writing compelling subject lines is crucial for improving open rates and engagement. Your subject line is the first thing recipients see, and it needs to grab their attention and entice them to open the email. Use clear, concise, and relevant language, and create curiosity or offer value to encourage opens.

Personalization is a powerful tool for creating engaging content. Use the recipient's name, past purchase behavior, and other relevant information to make your emails feel more tailored and relevant. Personalization not only improves engagement rates but also builds trust and loyalty with your audience.

Using dynamic content allows you to tailor different parts of your email to different segments of your audience. This can include personalized greetings, product recommendations, and targeted offers. By creating more relevant and engaging content, you can improve your email deliverability and build stronger connections with your audience.

Real-life examples of engaging content provide valuable insights into what works and what doesn't. For instance, a company that used personalized subject lines and dynamic content saw a significant increase in their open and click-through rates. These examples highlight the importance of understanding your audience and continuously optimizing your email content to meet their needs.

User-generated content can be a powerful way to engage your audience. Encourage your subscribers to share their experiences, reviews, and photos, and feature them in your emails. User-generated content not only adds authenticity to your emails but also builds a sense of community and encourages engagement.

Encouraging user-generated content involves creating opportunities for your audience to share their experiences and rewarding them for their contributions. Use social media, contests, and surveys to collect user-generated content, and feature it in your emails to create a more engaging and authentic experience.

Visuals play a significant role in engagement. Use images, videos, and infographics to make your emails more visually appealing and interesting. Visuals can help convey your message more effectively and make your content more engaging and memorable.

Using visuals effectively involves ensuring they are relevant to your content and aligned with your brand. Optimize your images and videos to reduce file sizes and ensure they load quickly. Include alt text for images to provide context for recipients who have images disabled, and use visuals to enhance your message and engage your audience.

Common content engagement mistakes include using spammy words, sending irrelevant content, and neglecting personalization. These practices can harm your sender reputation and increase the likelihood of your emails being marked as spam. By understanding and avoiding these mistakes, you can improve your email engagement and build stronger connections with your audience.

As we look ahead, it's important to stay informed about future trends in email marketing. The next chapter will explore emerging trends and technologies that can shape the future of email marketing, helping you stay ahead of the curve and continuously improve your email marketing strategy.

Chapter 10: Future Trends in Email Marketing

———

The evolution of email marketing is like an ever-changing landscape. Staying informed about emerging trends and technologies can help you stay ahead of the curve and continuously improve your email marketing strategy. This chapter will explore the future trends in email marketing, helping you stay ahead of the curve and achieve better results.

Email marketing has come a long way since its early days. From simple text-based emails to sophisticated, personalized campaigns, the industry has evolved significantly. As technology continues to advance, new trends and tools are emerging that can help you take your email marketing to the next level.

Current trends in email marketing include the rise of artificial intelligence (AI), increased personalization, and the use of interactive content. AI-powered tools can help you analyze data, optimize your campaigns, and create more personalized and relevant content. Interactive content, such as quizzes, polls, and interactive images, can make your emails more engaging and encourage higher levels of interaction.

The impact of AI on email marketing is significant. AI can help you analyze vast amounts of data, identify trends, and make data-driven decisions. It can also automate repetitive tasks, such as segmenting your email list, personalizing content, and optimizing send times. By leveraging AI, you can create more effective and efficient email marketing campaigns.

Using AI in email campaigns involves implementing tools and technologies that can analyze data, automate tasks, and optimize your strategy. Look for AI-powered email marketing platforms that offer features like predictive analytics, automated segmentation, and personalized content recommendations. By using AI, you can improve your email performance and achieve better results.

Machine learning is another important trend in email marketing. Machine learning algorithms can analyze data and learn from it, helping you identify patterns and trends that can inform your strategy. By using machine learning, you can create more personalized and relevant content, optimize your campaigns, and improve your email performance.

The future of email personalization involves using advanced data analysis and machine learning to create highly tailored and relevant content. This includes using data from multiple sources, such as browsing behavior, purchase history, and social media activity, to create a complete picture of each recipient and tailor your emails to their specific needs and preferences.

Staying ahead of personalization trends involves continuously learning and adapting your strategy. Use data and insights to inform your personalization efforts, and regularly test and optimize your content to ensure it remains relevant and engaging. By staying ahead of trends, you can create more effective and personalized email campaigns.

The impact of automation on email marketing is significant. Automation can help you streamline your email marketing efforts, saving time and resources while improving your results. Use automation to segment your email list, personalize content, and optimize send times. By leveraging automation, you can create more efficient and effective email marketing campaigns.

Creating interactive emails is an emerging trend that can make your content more engaging and encourage higher levels of interaction. Interactive emails can include elements like quizzes, polls, interactive images, and videos. These elements can make your emails more interesting and encourage recipients to engage with your content.

Designing for future trends involves staying informed about new technologies and best practices. Use responsive design to ensure your emails look good on all devices, and incorporate interactive elements to make your content more engaging. Regularly test and optimize your designs to ensure they remain effective and relevant.

The impact of privacy laws on email marketing is an important consideration for the future. As privacy regulations become stricter, it's essential to stay informed about legal requirements and ensure your practices are compliant. This includes obtaining explicit consent from subscribers, providing clear and transparent information about data usage, and honoring opt-out requests promptly.

Adapting to changing privacy laws involves regularly reviewing and updating your email marketing practices to ensure compliance. Stay informed about new regulations and consult with legal experts to ensure your practices meet legal requirements. By staying compliant, you can protect your business and build trust with your audience.

Data will continue to play a crucial role in future email marketing. Use data to inform your strategy, create personalized content, and optimize your campaigns. Regularly analyze your performance metrics and use the insights to make data-driven decisions. By leveraging data, you can create more effective and efficient email marketing campaigns.

The importance of omnichannel marketing will continue to grow. Integrating your email marketing efforts with other channels, such as social media, SMS, and web push notifications, can help you create a cohesive and consistent customer experience. Use data and insights from multiple channels to inform your email marketing strategy and create more personalized and relevant content.

Email deliverability will remain a critical focus for future email marketing. As spam filters and email providers continue to evolve, it's essential to stay informed about best practices and ensure your emails are optimized for deliverability. This includes using authentication protocols, maintaining a clean email list, and creating relevant and engaging content.

Improving future deliverability involves regularly testing and optimizing your emails, using data and insights to inform your strategy, and staying informed about changes in spam filters and email provider policies. By focusing on deliverability, you can ensure your emails reach your audience's inboxes and achieve your marketing goals.

Emerging technologies, such as augmented reality (AR) and virtual reality (VR), have the potential to revolutionize email marketing. These technologies can create immersive and interactive experiences, making your emails more engaging and memorable. Stay informed about emerging technologies and consider how they can be integrated into your email marketing strategy.

Preparing for future technologies involves staying informed about new developments, testing new tools and features, and continuously optimizing your strategy. Use data and insights to inform your decisions and ensure your emails remain relevant and engaging. By staying ahead of technological trends, you can create more effective and innovative email marketing campaigns.

As the landscape of email marketing continues to evolve, it's important to stay informed and adaptable. By understanding and leveraging future trends, you can create more effective and engaging email campaigns that resonate with your audience and achieve better results. Stay proactive, continuously optimize your strategy, and use data and insights to inform your decisions. This approach will help you stay ahead of the curve and achieve long-term email marketing success.

www.ingramcontent.com/pod-product-compliance
Lightning Source LLC
Chambersburg PA
CBHW030038230526
45472CB00002B/563

9 798328 503150